Disney · PIXAR

Cars

LET'S PARTY!

THINGS TO MAKE AND DO!

PaRragon

Bath · New York · Singapore · Hong Kong · Cologne · Delhi
Melbourne · Amsterdam · Johannesburg · Auckland · Shenzhen

CONTENTS

TIPS FOR SUCCESS

Remember, everything in this book should be made with the supervision and help of a grown up! A step labeled with "Kids" means that a child can do this step on their own. Some items will need to purchased from a supermarket or a craft/hobby store.

① Prepare your space

Cover your workspace with newspaper or a plastic or paper tablecloth. Make sure you and your children are wearing clothes (including shoes!) that you don't mind getting splattered with food, paint, or glue. But relax! You'll never completely avoid mess; in fact, it's part of the fun!

② Wash your hands

Wash your hands before starting a new project, and clean up as you go along. Clean hands make for clean crafts! Remember to wash hands afterwards too, using soap and warm water to remove any of the remaining materials.

③ Follow steps carefully

Follow each step carefully, and in the sequence in which it appears. We've tested all the projects; we know they work, and we want them to work for you, too.

4 Measure precisely

If a project gives you measurements, use your ruler, measuring cups, or measuring spoons to make sure you measure as accurately as you can. Sometimes, the success of the project may depend on it.

5 Be patient

You may need to wait while something bakes or allow paint, glue or clay to dry, sometimes for a few hours or even overnight. Be patient! Plan another activity while you wait, but it's important not to rush something as it may affect the outcome!

6 Clean up

When you've finished your project, clean up any mess. Store all the materials together so that they are ready for the next time you want to make and do. Remember it's a team effort!

CHECKERED RACE FLAG

Boost is always fast off the mark during a drifting race. Make this flag to host your own race at a party or just for fun!

YOU WILL NEED

THICK PAPER 28 X 40 INCHES

A PENCIL

A RULER

BLACK PAINT AND POT

SPONGE

A THIN STICK

TAPE

Kids 1

Divide a piece of white paper into squares with a pencil and ruler so you have a grid. Keep the pencil lines light – don't press too hard.

2

Cut a sponge to the same size as the squares. Dip the sponge into a pot of black paint and practice printing squares onto some newspaper (or scrap paper).

Kids 3

Print alternate black squares on the flag. Dip the sponge into paint for each new square. Dry.

Kids

4

Wrap the end of the flag around
a stick. Tape along the edge.
Start waving your race flag!

PISTON CUP TROPHY

The King has held a few trophies in his time. If you're a champ in the making, you'll need your very own trophy!

YOU WILL NEED

CARDBOARD BOX

PAPER – TO MAKE A TEMPLATE

SAFETY SCISSORS

PENCIL

RULER

GLUE

PAINT – GOLD, BLACK

1

Fold some paper 8 x 14 inches in half. See the picture above. Draw the shape onto the paper and then cut out the base and sides, to form the cup shape. Open the paper, you now have a symmetrical cup shape to draw around onto cardboard.

2

Draw one of the handle shapes and the cup base onto paper. Cut them out. Trace around your paper templates onto cardboard. You will need two handle shapes (facing opposite ways).

Glue the cut out card shapes together, as shown above. If there are any rough edges cover these with strips of masking tape.

Paint the cup in gold. Add two coats if necessary. Then add thin lines of black paint across the top of the cup, and paint the base black, leaving a gold area for the name plate.

THE KING'S TIP:
THIS IS A FUN ADDITION TO A PARTY. ONCE YOU HAVE PLAYED PARTY GAMES OR HELD A RACE THE WINNERS CAN POSE WITH THIS TROPHY!

READY, SET, GO! FRAME

Lightning knows all about photo finishes. Make this frame to capture all the racing action at a party or with your friends! Or use it as a decoration.

1

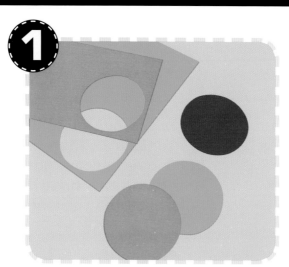

Draw three circles (about 5 inches in diameter) onto card stock. One red, one yellow, and one green. Cut them out.

YOU WILL NEED

- CARD STOCK
- COLORED PAPER
- SAFETY SCISSORS
- GLUE
- MASKING TAPE
- CUPS/LIDS - SOMETHING TO DRAW AROUND
- FOIL
- RIBBON

Kids 2

Glue the three circles on a piece of black card stock. Allow to dry.

Kids 3

Glue the traffic lights onto some card stock which you have covered with foil. Tape a piece of ribbon to the back.

4

Cut out three photos into circles, and glue them onto the traffic lights.

LIGHTNING'S TOP TIP: IF YOU ARE HOSTING A RACE-THEMED PARTY, THE PHOTOS OF RACE AND GAME WINNERS COULD BE PLACED INTO THIS FRAME FOR MOMENTS TO REMEMBER!

RACETRACK TABLETOP MANIA

Doc has raced on some very unique racetracks in his time. Create your own one-of-a-kind track below!

YOU WILL NEED

LARGE SHEETS OF PAPER

TAPE

PENS, PENCILS, CRAYONS

DOC'S TOP TIP: THIS IS A COOL WAY TO ADD SOME EXTRA RACING FUN TO A PARTY. MAKE THE TRACK THEN USE IT AS A TABLECLOTH!

1

Tape down large sheets of paper to cover a table. It will depend on the size of paper and size of table. Lightly outline a racetrack and a border in pencil.

Kids 2

Sit your friends around the table next to different areas of the racetrack. Go over the pencil lines with crayons or felt pens then add details like flags and banners.

3

Color the different areas of the racetrack. Big areas can be filled in quickly by rubbing big crayons on their side.

4

Add everyone's names around the edge of the track. Then admire your handy work like true racing pros.

MINI RACING FLAGS

Fillmore is a friendly car who loves to share. Make some yummy party food to share with your friends and rev it up with these cool mini racing flags!

YOU WILL NEED

PAPER

RULER

FELT PENS

TOOTHPICKS

GLUE

1

Cut out a paper rectangle 3 x 1 inches. Draw out a grid of small squares with a ruler and pencil.

Kids

2

Fill in the squares with a black felt pen, as shown above.

3

Fold the flag in half, then glue it onto a toothpick.

Try making other variations of flag designs. Push the flags into your party sandwiches.

RACING WHEELS

Guido and Luigi are tire experts, and they know some good tires when they see them...Like these!

YOU WILL NEED

PAPER

PENCIL

A ROLLING PIN

A COOKIE CUTTER

PENCIL OR TOOTHPICK - FOR MAKING HOLES

A BAKING TRAY

PAINTS

SALT DOUGH RECIPE:

2 CUPS PLAIN FLOUR

1 CUP OF SALT

1 CUP OF WATER

1 TABLESPOON OF COOKING OIL

1

Mix up 2 cups of plain flour and 1 cup of salt in a mixing bowl. Add 1 cup of water, and 1 tablespoon of oil to make a dough.

Kids
2

Knead the dough into a ball on a floured work surface. Roll it out to 1¼ inches thick. Cut out the wheel shapes using a cookie cutter.

3

Using the end of a pencil or paint brush, make a big whole in the middle of your wheel, then four smaller holes around the bigger hole. Leave the dough to dry, up to three days.

GUIDO AND LUIGI'S TIP:
IF YOU DON'T WANT TO HANG THESE UP, THEN YOU CAN LEAVE THEM ON YOUR TABLE TO USE AS COASTERS FOR YOUR PARTY DRINKS.

Paint the center of the wheels in a bright color, then outline this in black. Paint the outer wheel in black. Leave to dry. Thread the wheels onto string and hang up.

RACE CREW BADGES

Chick Hick's race crew plays an important role on race day. And it's just as important to know who everyone is! That's why you have badges!

YOU WILL NEED

CARD STOCK OR CRAFT FOAM

A PENCIL

PRINTED MESSAGES

GLUE AND CLEAR TAPE

PAINT

SAFETY PINS

CORRUGATED CARD

1

Print out some messages for your badges. Cut them out. Either use a printer or write out your messages on paper.

Kids

2

Brush black paint over corrugated card to create a patterned background. Draw and cut out other shapes from card, such as tools or lightning bolts.

3

Glue the printed messages onto the cut out card shapes.

CHICK HICK'S TOP TIP: EITHER GIVE THESE OUT AT YOUR PARTY OR PUT THEM INSIDE PARTY BAGS FOR YOUR FRIENDS TO TAKE HOME!

RACE TEAM MECHANIC

PIT STOP OFFICIAL

4

Tape a safety pin onto the back of each badge. Wear it with pride!

CHAMPION STORAGE

Sarge knows it's important to keep everything in order. That's why you need a cool box to keep your party stuff safe and organized before the main event!

Kids 1

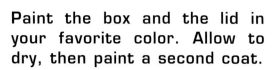

Paint the box and the lid in your favorite color. Allow to dry, then paint a second coat.

YOU WILL NEED

LARGE CARDBOARD BOX WITH LID

LARGE AND SMALL PAINTBRUSHES

ACRYLIC PAINTS

PENCIL

PAPER

SAFETY SCISSORS

WHITE GLUE AND BRUSH

2

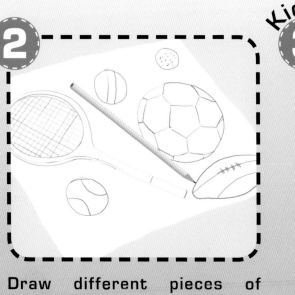

Draw different pieces of sports equipment (or whatever designs you wish) onto the white paper. Cut them out.

Kids 3

Use paints to color in the sports shapes.

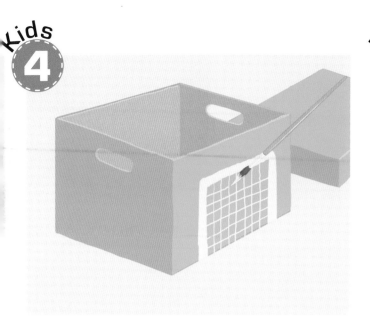

If you wish, paint a large white soccer net, or some other design onto the front of the box.

Arrange all the sports shapes around the box and glue them on.

SARGE'S TOP TIP:
THIS BOX SURE IS NEAT. ONCE YOU'VE THROWN A PARTY YOU CAN USE IT AGAIN AND AGAIN!

STARS OF CARS COOKIES

Ramone loves stars, flames, or lightning bolts. In fact, anything that stands out! Make these funky shaped cookies and wow your friends!

YOU WILL NEED

- LARGE MIXING BOWL
- SIFTER
- 2 ¼ CUPS ALL-PURPOSE FLOUR
- PINCH OF SALT
- 1 TEASPOON BAKING POWDER
- 1 TABLESPOON BUTTER
- ¾ CUP LIGHT BROWN SUGAR
- 2 EGGS, BEATEN
- 2 OUNCES CORN SYRUP
- 3 OUNCES CHOCOLATE BAR
- ROLLING PIN
- A COOKIE CUTTER
- NONSTICK COOKING SPRAY
- BAKING SHEET

1

Pre-heat the oven to 325°F. Sift the flour, salt, and baking powder into a large bowl.

Kids 2

With your fingers, rub the butter into the dry ingredients. Add the sugar. In a cup, stir together the eggs and the corn syrup.

Kids 3

With a wooden spoon, beat the ingredients until they are thoroughly combined. Break the chocolate into small chunks and add to the mixture.

4

5

Place the dough on a board. Sprinkle it lightly with flour so it doesn't stick to the rolling pin. Roll out the dough until it's about ½-inch thick. With a cookie cutter, cut out the cookies, like these star-shaped cookies.

Lightly grease a baking sheet with nonstick cooking spray or vegetable oil. Place the cookies about 2 inches apart on the baking sheet. Bake for about 15 minutes, until golden. Allow to cool.

RAMONE'S TOP TIP:
EXPERIMENT WITH DIFFERENT COOKIE SHAPES JUST LIKE I EXPERIMENT WITH MY PAINT DESIGNS!

PARTY CARS

Mater is a cheery character and full of surprises. Give these party cars to all your friends and family, they hold some unexpected treats and fun!

YOU WILL NEED

- CARDBOARD TUBES
- SAFETY SCISSORS
- PAINT
- BLACK, RED, AND YELLOW CARD STOCK
- PAPER FASTENERS
- GLUE
- PARTY GIFTS – CANDY, BADGES, BALLOONS, ETC

1

Paint a cardboard tube and allow it to dry. Cut out four wheels from black card, then glue smaller red circles to the middle of each wheel. Cut out a steering wheel.

2

Cut along the tube and make a rectangular hole in the middle. Glue a steering wheel inside. Add decoration either in paint or add shapes made from card, such as lightning bolts.

3

Make four holes in the tube where you want the wheels to go. Attach the wheels to the tube using paper fasteners.

Wrap a few small gifts/candy into a piece of tissue paper. Twist the ends so the gifts won't fall out, then push inside the tube.

MATER'S TOP TIP:
YOU COULD WRITE YOUR FRIENDS' NAMES ON THEIR CARS FOR A SUPER SPECIAL FINISHING TOUCH!

RACING PLANES

Blimp always has a birdseye view of every race. Now your friends can soar through the air, too! Try making these for some cool party games.

Kids 1

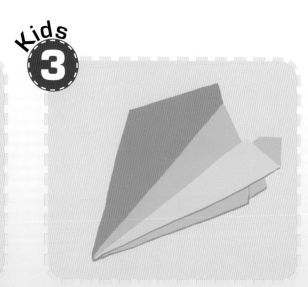

Fold the sheet of paper in half. Turn down the corners at one end so that the folded-down edges line up along your fold.

YOU WILL NEED

SQUARE SHEET OF COLORED PAPER

STAPLER AND STAPLES

ROUND STICKERS OR PAINT FOR DECORATION

Kids 2

To make the wings, fold the top down again, lining it up along the bottom of the shape. Repeat on the other side.

Kids 3

Fold the top flaps down again, lining them up along the bottom of the airplane.

Open out the folds that you made in the last step. To help the plane fly better, put two staples in the folded layers near the nose. Decorate the plane with round stickers on the wings and sides.

BLIMP'S TIP:
THE TRIANGULAR FLAPS AT THE WING BASES WILL MAKE THE PLANE FLY IN DIFFERENT DIRECTIONS. FOLD THEM UP IF YOU WANT THE PLANE TO DO AN INSIDE LOOP AND DOWN FOR AN OUTSIDE LOOP.

FLO'S BURGERS

Flo knows how to cook up a storm in her café. Here's a special recipe that she has cooked up just for you and your party, come rain or shine!

YOU WILL NEED

TO MAKE 4 BURGERS:

VEGETABLE OIL

1 SMALL ONION, CHOPPED

1 TEASPOON CHOPPED PARSLEY (OR HERB OF CHOICE)

½ CUP BREADCRUMBS

8-OUNCE CAN RED SALMON

OR TUNA PACKED WITH WATER

1 EGG

SALT AND PEPPER TO TASTE

FLOUR

LETTUCE, TOMATO SLICES, ONION RINGS, MAYONNAISE

4 WHOLE WHEAT BURGER BUNS

PAN

Heat two teaspoonfuls of oil in the pan; add the onion, herbs, and breadcrumbs and sauté gently for five minutes.

Kids

Pour the mixture into a bowl and let cool. Add the fish, egg, salt, and pepper. Mix everything together with your hands.

Kids

Sprinkle some flour onto the work surface and shape the mixture into burgers.

4 Wash and dry the pan, add oil, and place over medium heat. Fry the burger for five minutes on each side.

Kids 5 Put each burger on a bun and garnish with lettuce, tomato slices, onion rings, and mayonnaise.

FLO'S TIP:
SERVE THESE TASTY TREATS ON YOUR RACETRACK TABLETOP, WITH WHEEL DECORATIONS AND MINI CHECKERED FLAGS!

RACE BOATS

For more party game fun, hit the water with these sailboats and race your boat across the finish line.

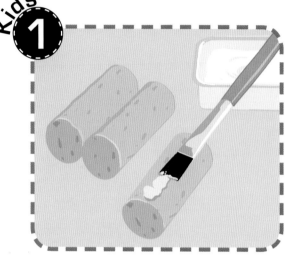

Kids 1

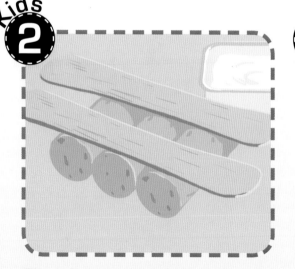

Glue the corks together, side by side. Let dry.

YOU WILL NEED

FOR EACH BOAT:

3 CORKS

WHITE GLUE AND BRUSH

2 ICE-CREAM STICKS

TOOTHPICK

SCRAPS OF COLORED PAPER

Kids 2

Glue the two sticks to the top of the corks as shown. Let dry.

3

Cut a triangular sail from some colored paper. Apply a little glue to the tip of the sail and wrap it around the top of the toothpick to make a mast. Let dry.

4

Make a hole in the center of the middle cork between the sticks. Push the toothpick mast into the hole. Bend the sail so it sits on the top of the boat.

5

Cut a tiny triangle in yellow paper and glue to the top of the toothpick mast to make a flag.

LIGHTNING'S TOP TIP: ADD THESE LIGHTNING FLASHES USING FABRIC PAINT TO MAKE YOUR SAILBOATS LOOK EXTRA COOL.

TRUCKER HAT

Mack is always wearing his stylish trucker hat wherever he goes. To get noticed at your party try making your own. Lookin' good!

Kids 1

Outline the eye area and lightning bolts in pencil, then fill them in with a brush using white and yellow paint. Leave to dry. Dip a cork into some blue paint. Carefully press the cork onto the white area to print blue circles for the eyes. Leave to dry.

YOU WILL NEED

A PLAIN RED BASEBALL CAP

AN OLD TOWEL OR T-SHIRT TO COVER YOURSELF

PENCIL

PAINTS – FABRIC PAINT IS

PREFERABLE

BRUSH

PERMANENT MARKER PEN/ FABRIC PEN

A CORK

COTTON SWABS

Kids 3

Add orange dots to the lightning bolt with a cotton swab and then add white paint to highlight the pupils.

2

Add black pupils to the eyes with a marker pen and outline the whole of the white eye area and lightning bolt in black.